The East India Company

A Captivating Guide to the English Company That Was Created for the Exploitation of Trade with East and Southeast Asia and India

Free Bonus from Captivating History (Available for a Limited time)

Hi History Lovers!

Now you have a chance to join our exclusive history list so you can get your first history ebook for free as well as discounts and a potential to get more history books for free! Simply visit the link below to join.

Captivatinghistory.com/ebook

Also, make sure to follow us on Facebook, Twitter and Youtube by searching for Captivating History.

Contents

Introduction

Imagine, if you will, a typical day at your office. Or rather, a typical day of you getting to your office. You stand up, have breakfast, hug your spouse and your child, and then hug your elderly father; he still has those scars from working in the coalmine for 25 years on that one hand that lands softly on your cheek, telling you how proud he is that you've become a chief business officer of that massive corporate branch in your city. And you can't help but feel proud, too, since you came from nothing and have worked hard to get to where you are, unlike some of your colleagues who got there through a few connections and a few well-placed bribes. But you don't care about that now; you have a cab to catch.

As the cab drives slowly down the main road, you spot a few high school senior girls taking selfies. Two of them, whiter than snow, are wearing kimonos and excessive makeup. Their friend, an Indian girl that appears a bit younger, is decked in the typical Western gear—jeans, a flashy shirt, a pair of Converse All Star sneakers, and a hat with an American Eagle logo on it. They are joined by two black girls, both wearing saris, and you giggle as the Indian girl attempts to fix the sari of one of the newcomers. They all look extremely cheerful. Must be the end of the semester or a local festival.

Some noise interrupts you on your drive, as you see a group of protesters clashing with a group of counter-protesters. They are in front of that old theater where a fancy actor's group from London is going to stage *Hamlet* tonight. Upon close inspection, you see that the two groups are the Westboro Baptist Church and the Black Hebrew Israelites. You're not particularly interested in what they have to shout at each other, so you roll up the window. The corporate office is nearby anyway.

Once you enter the building, you're greeted by your colleagues. From what you can tell, at least forty percent of them weren't even born in this country, and an additional fifty percent aren't even from this city. But you don't care. Their merit speaks for themselves, and your meeting is about to start.

The early 21st century is no stranger to these situations, to different cultures either clashing or embracing, to conglomerates being an amazing place for business opportunities but also a hotbed for corruption, to people becoming wealthy despite coming from humble beginnings, to theater plays originating in countries an ocean apart being performed in your own backyard. But interestingly, this is not a new phenomenon. In fact, over 400 years ago, it was more or less the norm in the Indian subcontinent.

For years, the topic of the East India Company has fascinated historians as well as economists, anthropologists, sociologists, and other scholarly types. Some regard the Company as a prime example of an empire draining the resources of underprivileged people and destroying their entire cultures in a heartbeat. Others see it as the earliest corporate business enterprise and a precursor to modern capitalism. But with 258 years of activity, the East India Company can't really be defined in these simple terms. It's all of them yet so much more. And within this volume, we'd like to introduce the fascinating world of the EIC to you, with all of its bits and bobs and as uncut as possible. We'll get to meet some of the fascinating people that shaped the Company, from various Indian royalty to different British servants of the EIC, as well as its detractors on both sides of the Eurasian landmass. But more importantly, we'll get to see what made the petty English merchants embark upon the journey to the East and what made the Company rise from a trading business to a semi-independent country. And, consequently, what made it fall.

The flag of the British East India Company[i]

https://commons.wikimedia.org/wiki/File:Flag_of_the_British_East_India_Company_(1801).svg

Chapter 1 – The Company's First Century: Establishment and Growth of the EIC, Rivals, and Issues

The Earliest Days of the EIC

What we know today as the East India Company was officially formed on December 31st, 1600, when Queen Elizabeth I issued a charter that allowed the Company Merchants of London to trade in the East Indies. At the time, England wasn't a wealthy nation. A little over a decade before the formation of the EIC, the English had suffered massive defeats against the mighty Spanish Armada. In terms of naval power, they were nowhere near their direct trading competitors. For example, the Dutch, the Portuguese, and even the French had a lot more naval strength, and they were also already trading across the ocean. In other words, the formation of this new company was a massive risk on England's part.

During its formation, the Company had a relatively strict hierarchical structure. After receiving the charter from Queen Elizabeth, the EIC had the monopoly (among the English traders and existing companies, at least) to trade in the Indian Ocean exclusively. The Company was run by 24 directors, who were, in turn, presided over by a governor and his deputy. These directors would be elected by the body known as the General Court, which was made up of different influential investors and subscribers to the Company. It's fascinating to point out that the English weren't the only members of the General Court. At times, even foreign investors like the Dutch would purchase stock in the Company and get involved with the election process. As the 18th century rolled out, there was even a good deal of women investors, including royalty.

In terms of lower ranks, there was a grand total of four. The lowest station a man (or a woman, though the vast majority of Company workers were men) could hold within the EIC was that of a writer. After five years in the Company's service, a writer could be promoted to a factor. Three more years, and he would become a junior merchant, and an additional three years would earn him the senior merchant position. The annual salary, of course, varied between these four: 5 pounds for writers, 15 pounds for factors, 30 pounds for junior merchants, and 40 pounds for senior merchants. Of course, if you were to leave the Company's service, you would receive no pension.

Each rank had different duties within the Company. Writers, for example, would get the lowest jobs, which, as their name suggests, largely constituted of administrative paperwork. They would maintain trade logs, file reports, maintain copies of the Company's many contracts, etc. A factor would be an executive of a factory, who would be in charge of direct trade and the factory's maintenance. Back in the day, the term "factory" referred to the European mercantile establishments in India and Southeast Asia where they would conduct trade. Junior and senior merchants performed extensive trade, and if you reached the rank of senior merchant, you were a viable candidate for the position of a director or, later on, a governor. However, reaching these positions wasn't easy; most of the Company's writers were between fifteen and nineteen years old, and life expectancy, at the time, was, at best, thirty. In addition, the median expectancy of working for the Company was a meager three years. The reason behind these low numbers is the high chance of death among the EIC employees, as well as a high probability of dismissals among every rank.

As early as 1601, the English had set sail for the Spice Islands, and the first voyage was led by James Lancaster aboard the ship called the *Red Dragon*. The very next year, the Dutch would form their own East India Company, known as the *Vereenigde Oostindische Compagnie*, or VOC. The Dutch would prove to be a strong competitor to the EIC, even at this early stage of its existence, but they were nowhere near as prominent as the Portuguese. During the late 16th and early 17th centuries, the Portuguese East India Company had a virtual monopoly on trade in the Indian Ocean. In fact, they could even capture and loot English and Dutch ships and legally keep the spoils. Other merchants either had to buy a trading license from them (called a *cartaz*) or fight tooth and nail for their survival.

Trips to the East Indies were horrific at this early stage of the EIC's existence. For example, a goldsmith named Anthony Marlowe documented one such journey in 1607 when the ship he was on, called the *Hector*, was on its way to the port of Surat. The *Hector* was one of three ships that went on this journey, alongside the more famous *Red Dragon* and a third ship named *Consent*. Marlowe goes into a lot of detail, describing how the mariners dealt with problems, how they traded, fought off threats, and navigated extremely dangerous ocean waters on their way to their destination. It's interesting to learn, for example, about their encounters with certain African locals. Namely, after they had complained that a crew member committed some crimes against them, the ship's captain and a few other officers found the man and punished him, dispensing justice. Of course, the English and the Africans were far from respecting people of races other than their own in the 17th century, but this act does show that human interactions were just as complex back then as they are now. Of course, there are more examples of this documented in Marlowe's journal. At one point, he mentioned that there were some known criminals aboard the ship and that a steward would lose his position if he were to commit a crime aboard any of the ships or on land. But he also mentioned that some criminals were reinstated as stewards, showing that either the captain could practice leniency or that there weren't enough crew members and that the captain had to think in terms of practicality. Marlowe also noted each important death upon the ship and even recalled, with lamentation, the Portuguese treatment of the Africans, as well as his own crewmembers.

Voyages like these, however, were not all doom and gloom. For example, the crew of the *Red Dragon* actually staged some of Shakespeare's plays, like *Hamlet* and *Richard III*, in 1607 while they were on the island of Socotra and at Sierra Leone. Historically speaking, these were the first productions of Shakespeare's works outside of Europe, and they were performed when the bard was very much alive and well. Marlowe himself wrote about festive dinners the crew would sometimes have and how well the trade would go at times.

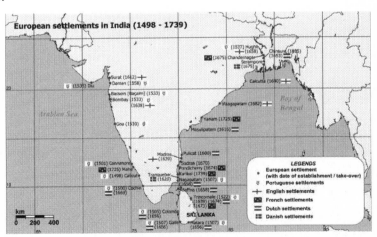

European settlements on the Indian Subcontinent between 1498 and 1739[ii]

The Company's Rivals and Early Issues

Even during the first decade, the EIC was facing different trade problems. It wasn't just the Portuguese racket that disturbed their business. In fact, the market had already been cluttered with traders from other parts of the world, such as China, Arabia, and even from powerful Indian states. One move that actually helped the EIC grow at a decent rate was the fact that it was a joint-stock company. In a joint-stock company, every single member can contribute to the capital and, as a result of that, earn lots of revenue in the form of various dividends. Most of their rivals, including even the smaller traders from England, were regulated companies, where revenue was enjoyed directly by the members of that company and nobody else (of course, they were also the only ones to suffer losses in case of mismanagement).

During these years, the Company merchants had to learn via trial and error. For example, in 1603, Lancaster brought a lot of pepper back to England from his trades in the East Indies. While there was now an abundance of pepper in the kingdom, the market was glutted, and the prices dropped. In other words, people who traded goods from the East had to be extremely careful when it came to regulating the quantity of the goods they sold. Another good example of the Company learning on its feet is the use of ships. In the first few decades, the merchants would buy and own ships, but the repairs were costly to the point where they became an economic risk. For the vast majority of the Company's existence, they would hire ships instead. And then there's the trade itself. Because of their many different trading rivals, the English couldn't earn enough money from trading across the sea. However, intra-country trade with other Asian territories (like China and many different Indian states, for instance) proved especially lucrative, so the Company focused a lot of its efforts there.

However, intra-country trade had its own set of drawbacks. In the early 17th century, the dominant political force in the region was the

Islamic Mughal Empire. Throughout the next hundred or so years, they would almost conquer the entirety of the Indian subcontinent, which gave them the power to subjugate every minor state nearby. The Company's relationship with the Mughal Empire would become a complex one, but during these early days, it had to "play nice." In 1615, Sir Thomas Roe became the Company's ambassador at the Mughal court. This was a huge step forward for the English, considering that just two years prior, they had established their first factory in Surat.

Roe, during his service, was not unaware of what the English had to deal with during the early days of the Company. It wasn't that long ago that they had to fight two devastating wars against the Portuguese, both around Surat. The first was in 1613, with Sir Thomas Best as the commander, which didn't end up being a victory for the British; however, it did bring about the factory's formation at Surat. However, it was the second war in 1615, with Nicholas Downton commanding the English troops, that marked the decisive victory over the Portuguese forces. Roe, an Englishman, clearly supported his countrymen, but he nevertheless urged against any land wars in Asia, mainly because wars were far from cost-effective, and there were extreme risks that could damage the business.

Surat, a port in western India, had one of the two major Company factories, with the second being in Bantam, located in western Java. Factors from Surat largely exported cheap textiles but sometimes traded indigo and saltpeter. Bantam, on the other hand, was the center of the pepper trade. These two became official centers (also known as presidencies) of the early Company whom all later, minor subordinate factories reported to. Each factory was run by a president, though they were called "chiefs" before 1618.

It's interesting to see just how ambitious the English merchants were at the time. For example, their trade was booming in both the Indian subcontinent and in what would later be known as Indochina and the Malay Archipelago. However, they also tried establishing factories in Thailand, Malaysia, and even Japan. Curiously enough, both the

French East India Company and the VOC also contacted the Japanese in order to establish their factories there. However, in terms of the EIC, none of these plans came to fruition.

Before 1662, most members of the Company didn't engage in intra-country trade. In fact, the Company specifically prohibited the practice so that all of the proceeds could go in-house. However, ship captains and Company factors still engaged in trading within the Asian countries, earning a lot of money and purchasing luxury goods such as porcelain and diamonds. Considering they couldn't stop this, when 1662 came around, the EIC had lifted the ban and allowed everyone to trade as long as they didn't interfere with the Company's business.

The 1660s saw a few other notable changes within the Company. For example, in 1631, a massive famine struck Surat. This problem, as well as a few others, saw the Company shift its business to other towns and establish factories there, such as Bombay and Bengal. Bombay itself was given to King Charles II of England by the Portuguese. However, he relinquished it to the Company in 1668 because he could not find the funds to manage it properly. In 1687, Bombay would become the EIC's center of trade instead of Surat.

Interestingly, Surat wasn't the earliest factory the Company formed in the Indian subcontinent. In fact, in 1611, they had traded at the port of Masulipatnam on India's southeastern coast (also known as the Coromandel Coast). However, in the late 1680s, the Mughal Empire annexed the local Muslim kingdom of Golconda, which included the port town of Masulipatnam. Worried about the trade, the Company moved most of its operations to a neighboring factory at Madras. We should note that the Madras factory was established in 1639 and that, by the 1680s, it had thrived so much that it had eclipsed Surat in the textile trade. Madras itself would be surpassed by a different factory based in Bengal, or, to be more specific, based in Calcutta. In fact, Calcutta itself became a hub for the rich Englishmen in the East India Company, and today we have many firsthand accounts of just how lively and agreeable life was for the average wealthy merchant. It was like a small yet bustling English community outside of mainland England.

The End of the Century and the EIC

The end of the century was marked by a few major events. First, there was the so-called Child's War (also known as the First Anglo-Mughal War), which lasted from 1686 to 1690. A few company officials, most notably the governor of the EIC, Josiah Child, wanted a fortified Bengal settlement and, more importantly, for the Mughals to treat them as a sovereign state so they could grant the EIC trading privileges. The war ended with a decisive Mughal victory and a peace treaty in February 1690, with Emperor Aurangzeb allowing the English to trade as long as they paid fines and returned the goods they had seized.

The Company also had to deal with the Dutch encroaching on their business. The two forces had faced off against each other in several naval wars over the course of the past few decades, and in 1682, the Company had to abandon their pepper factory in Bantam. Because of that, the merchants had to focus on the textile trade exclusively. Of course, this trade had already been extremely lucrative for the Company merchants; they would normally export calico cotton, which was cheap to produce, soft, and, unlike wool, could be dyed in elaborate colors. This fabric became so popular in England that Parliament actually issued ludicrous laws that prohibited wearing anything other than wool, and it even went so far as them banning people from burying their dead in anything other than wool garments. However, the trade continued to boom, and in the early 18th century, the Parliament allowed the use of cotton—as long as it wasn't imported.

From these examples, we can see that the English governing body at the time didn't openly support the Company, at least not uniformly. There were Parliament members, lords, and other nobles who had shares within the EIC, but more than a few prominent figures (including the famous author Daniel Defoe) openly criticized the

Company's practices. Their major point of contention was that the Company merchants exported more silver and gold out of the country to the Asian market than they brought back to England. In a now-famous speech, John Pollexfen, a Parliament member in 1695, declared that companies (such as the EIC) had bodies but no souls and, therefore, had no consciences. It's incredible to think that Pollexfen's criticism of joint-stock companies like the EIC perfectly mirrors modern-day criticisms of multinational conglomerates and corporations.

But possibly one of the biggest problems that the early Company had to deal with came from the so-called "interlopers," or free agents who traded in the same waters as the Company ships. Namely, the Company wasn't the only mercantile body to get trading charters from the English royalty. As early as 1604, a former Company employee, Sir Edward Michelborne, got permission from King James I of England to trade in the Indian Ocean. Richard Penkvell, an adventurer and an aspiring merchant, also got permission in 1607. All of these independent merchants began to pop up roughly around the time when the first public criticisms of the EIC were emerging. One such example includes the book *The Trades Increase* by a gentleman called Robert Kayll. His criticisms were actually broadly addressing the practices of all companies, but he didn't choose the title *The Trades Increase* for no reason; *Trades Increase* was the name of a popular Company ship at the time.

Kayll was far from being the earliest critic of the Company, and Pollexfen was far from being the last. Nearly all of their criticisms focused on a few broad points. For example, they attacked the Company's massive export of bullion (i.e., gold and silver) to Asia, which amounted to over 750,000 pounds by 1623. In addition, they focused on the monopoly the Company supposedly held over other English merchants. Company merchants, such as Dudley Digges and Thomas Mun, worked hard on their rebuttals of the criticisms hurled at the Company by people like Kayll, but their successes varied, and besides, the damage had already been done. In 1615, Parliament issued a ban on exporting gold and silver. While it's true that the Company was practically the only exception to this new law, this move was still a massive blow to their economic growth. But the constant encroachment of interlopers on the Company's trade was a far greater threat. In 1635, Sir William Courten got his own permission to trade in Company waters, which was then passed down to his son, who was also named William. Courten's association was called "Adventurers to Goa and Other Parts," and though it had only survived for less than a decade, it struck a significant blow to the EIC by simply existing.

The next two decades saw the rise and fall of Oliver Cromwell and the restoration of the English monarchy, but more importantly, it was during these years that the king of England would provide a charter to the EIC that allowed it to go to war with any of its neighbors, an important legal detail that would have extremely long-lasting consequences. And as the late 1680s and early 1690s came, with the Glorious Revolution taking place and William of Orange being installed as king, the Company was in a bind. More than a few of their detractors were members of the British Parliament, and the Company had to bribe their way into getting their charter renewed in 1693. As corrupt as that sounds, it was far from being the first time the Company actually dabbled in such deeds. Several past rulers were getting annual payments from the Company, and during the early days, the directors also frequently engaged in tax fraud.

But none of that corruption and none of the money could have stopped the inevitable. In 1698, a new joint-stock company was formed, which provided a two-million-pound loan to the government. The so-called English Company (or the New Company) had one advantage that their older counterpart didn't have, which was domestic political support. However, Parliament made one crucial error. Namely, they allowed the Old Company to settle its affairs within three years but allowed their merchants to invest in shares of the New Company. With years of mercantile experience, the Old Company invested 315,000 pounds into their new rival's shares, which pretty much allowed them to survive indefinitely. For the next decade, the two companies would compete for power, but it was clear that there would be no definite winner. The Old Company still had lots of connections with Asian traders and a well-established route, not to mention a whole century of experience in overseas trade. The two entities would ultimately merge into one on April 22nd, 1709, and would bear the name of the United Company of Merchants of England. However, at the end of the Company's first century, its future was still uncertain.

Chapter 2 – The Company's Second Century: Growth and Expansion, Trade with China, Financial Crises, and "Statehood"

Aggressive Policies of the EIC

In 1717, Mughal Emperor Farrukhsiyar issued a *ferman*, also spelled as *firman* (an imperial order), that allowed the Company to trade in the empire's territory without having to pay any customs. It was only eight years after the Old and the New Company had merged into one, and this event was, without a doubt, one of the earliest successes that this brand-new EIC had achieved. The Company servants slowly saw an increase in trade, but a little over two decades later, they would begin to pursue a much more aggressive approach toward their trading rivals and the neighboring states on the Indian peninsula.

Europe of the mid-17th century was plagued with wars. Because of Britain siding with specific allies during these European wars, France became one of its most bitter rivals, and they would soon go to war themselves. Naturally, since both the British and the French had their own East India Companies and their own Company establishments in India and Southeast Asia, clashes were inevitable. The harshest of these were the so-called Carnatic Wars, which were three successive military clashes between the British, the French, and the Mughals on the southeast coast of modern India. Each of the three wars massively depleted the warring sides, and victories were hard-won, but with the conclusion of the Third Carnatic War (1756-1763), it was clear that the British would come out on top. These wars saw the early military achievements of Robert Clive, a British officer who would rise to the rank of commander-in-chief and who came to be known as "Clive of India." The British also saw victories at the Battle of Wandiwash in 1760, as well as the Siege of Pondicherry, the last remaining French Indian outpost, in 1761. While the French were allowed to trade after the Treaty of Paris in 1763 and eventually regained control of Pondicherry as per the treaty's terms, they would never be the powerful traders they were before the Carnatic Wars.

Nearly all of these events pointed to one conclusion as far as the Company servants were concerned—the EIC needed an army, and they needed it badly. In 1756, a local ruler (or nawab) called Siraj-ud-Daulah attacked and conquered Calcutta, bringing unrest and panic to the Company-held Bengal region. The largest stationed British force at the time was in Madras, so the Company sent them, with Robert Clive in charge, to retake Bengal. The British, of course, had full permission from Parliament to engage in wars of conquest thanks to the charter from the 1680s. Clive retook Bengal in 1757, and on June 23rd of that same year, he crushed Siraj-ud-Daulah at the village of Plassey. One of Clive's collaborators and a general who betrayed Siraj-ud-Daulah on that day, Mir Jafar, would come to rule the former nawab's position.

Of course, the Company didn't maintain good relations with Mir Jafar. Though he had come to rely on the EIC, at one point, he refused to compensate them for the huge sums of money they demanded from him. As a result of that, he was forced to abdicate, and the Company installed a new nawab, his son-in-law, Mir Qasim. But Mir Qasim himself wanted independence from the British, so he fled to the western state of Awadh and allied himself to Awadh's nawab, Shuja-ud-Daula. The emperor of Mughal, Shah Alam II, also joined them in their cause against the Company, which had instated Mir Jafar once again as the nawab of Bengal. However, Mir Jafar was old and died soon after, which led to the ascension of his teenaged and inexperienced son, Najm-ud-Daulah, in 1764. October of that very same year would see the East India Company clash against Mir Qasim's tripartite alliance at Buxar, where the Indian alliance suffered a humiliating defeat. As a result, and according to the Treaty of Allahabad, the Company gained control over Bengal, Orissa, and Bihar indefinitely. These three territories had more people than all of Britain combined at the time, and the Company had just received complete control to do whatever they wanted over them. Needless to say, the victory at Buxar was a moment of absolute triumph for the EIC.

The internal structure of the Company changed with the new expansionist policies of its directors. Aside from writers, directors could also assign cadets, who were junior members of the Company's military divisions. Even nominating writers and cadets would earn the Company seniors hefty sums of money, and up until the 1800s, there were no entrance exams, and they could name anyone to these positions. Needless to say, nepotism and corruption came to dominate the Company's upper echelon during this period.

Statue of Robert Clive, King Charles Street, London, UK[iii]

The EIC's Many Crises and Parliament's Involvement

It was this period between the 1760s and the 1790s that was riddled with crisis after crisis within (and outside of) the Company. Critics such as Thomas Pownall and Adam Smith would go after the EIC using the old arguments of monopoly and corruption, but with the added component of statehood, they had new ammunition to hurl at the Company's officials. According to Smith, the Company could not act as both a ruler of local Indian lands and as a trading giant with a monopoly in Indian waters because the two positions were inherently contradictory. A ruler would have to allow competition to boost trade and increase the economy, while the Company's monopoly did the exact opposite of that. In addition, the critics focused on the condition of the EIC's new territories, citing the famine that struck Bengal in 1769, the taxation practices of the

Company in this region, and the lack of silver currency. Madras, in particular, was a hotbed of corruption, with the famous case of Muhammad Ali Khan, the nawab of Arcot, convincing the Company's officials to attack the region of Tanjore and annex it to his territory in exchange for his debt repayment, which was enormous at the time. Not only did this act prompt violence and infighting within the Company itself, but it further alienated the EIC from the British Parliament, the British general public, and the Indian locals.

In 1773, Parliament would pass the so-called Regulating Act. This document was a historic moment in the Company's existence, but it was not necessarily made in its benefit. Thanks to this document, Calcutta (and by extension Bengal) became the de facto center of all EIC dealings, with higher-ups from Madras and Bombay having to report to it. The Company also had a supreme court presided over by four judges. But most importantly, Calcutta (and effectively the EIC) would be run by a governor-general, a position that was first held by Warren Hastings in 1774. We'll delve more into Hastings in a later chapter.

Another act, known as the India Act, was passed in 1783 under Prime Minister William Pitt. The reason behind this act was Parliament wanted more direct control over the Company's dealings. While the directors would still retain their rights to trade and to do business as they saw fit, the Parliament-issued Board of Control in London was now pulling all of the strings. The India Act also gave the governor-general more direct power than before, but he was also not particularly influential when compared to this new board. Up until 1811, Henry Dundas would be effectively running the Board of Control, despite its democratic structure (it was to contain one secretary of state, one chancellor of the exchequer, and four members of the Privy Council, which was a formal body of advisors to the king).

Calcutta in the 17th century, from "Cassell's Illustrated History of England, Volume"
by John Cassell, 1865[iv]

https://commons.wikimedia.org/wiki/File:P615_Calcutta_in_the_17th_Century.jpg

Expansion Efforts of the EIC

When it held power over the land, the EIC would extract money from the local peasants through the middlemen known as zamindars. It was a simple system: the peasants would sell their produce to the zamindars, the zamindars would take their cut, and the rest of the money went to the Company. However, with the new army and mounting financial crises, the Company wanted to squeeze as much money out of the peasants as possible, especially when they would acquire new territories through warfare. They had to approach this problem carefully, of course, since both the peasants and the zamindars could rebel at the slightest hint of oppression.

But the Company was about to receive an interesting solution that would shift the relations between the locals to nobody's advantage other than the EIC. In the 1790s, Charles Cornwallis sailed to India and became the new governor-general of the Company. As early as 1793, he issued something called the Permanent Settlement. According to this document, the zamindars, who held no land before and were merely collecting revenue for the Company, were now expected to become landowners and pay their superiors a fixed sum of money per year. This action made the peasants nothing more than tenants of their own land, but more importantly, the zamindars couldn't pay the amount that the Company set for them. The Permanent Settlement itself didn't produce the financial results that the Company wanted, which is why a series of additional settlements were issued in different parts of the EIC's territories.

Trading with China

Most people tend to connect Britain and China via an event called the Opium Wars. For decades, the British would "export" opium to Chinese lands close to the Company's Indian territories, while the Chinese authorities would try to put a stop to it. From instituting sales restrictions in the 1760s to the outright ban on the opium trade via the Canton Edict in 1799, followed by a large-scale trade prohibition on opium in 1839, China tried its best to keep the Company's opium out of the country. However, what most people don't realize is that the opium trade was intimately connected to the tea and sugar trade in the 18th century.

Tea used to be an expensive commodity in Britain, but ever since Thomas Garway began to sell it from his coffee house in Exchange Alley in London, it began to soar in popularity. He advertised the beverage as a cure-all and an amazing stimulant, better than coffee, and the public wanted more. Considering the Company's position in Southeast Asia, they were in the best possible position to flood the market with tea and earn a great deal of money. But it wasn't just tea that they sold. Roughly around the same time, sugar exports became equally popular, since most people who consumed tea did so with sugar.

However, getting tea required a vibrant trade with China, and thanks to annexing regions around the modern-day cities of Patna and Benares, the Company had the perfect commodity for the Chinese consumers in the form of opium. The Chinese wouldn't buy any other products from the Europeans other than opium and cotton, which the EIC also readily traded. However, the opium trade was a far steadier way of earning a stable income than the cotton trade. With the opium trade restrictions in the 1760s, the Company merchants had to resort to smuggling, which proved every bit as lucrative as the legal sales of the substance. In fact, it was so lucrative that the Company established a monopoly on selling opium in 1773 and another monopoly on growing and producing it in 1797, two years prior to the Canton Edict.

Lovers of history usually ignore the tea and sugar trade and focus entirely on the opium trade and the subsequent wars it led to. But it's extremely interesting to know that because of opium, tea had become a cultural phenomenon in the United Kingdom, and it remains a huge part of the everyday lives of the British public even today. Not only was it one of the cheapest drinks in the kingdom itself (it was cheaper than locally brewed beer), but it was a great stimulant that you could easily brew anywhere. It's only fitting that its rise to popularity came from something as heinous as the opium trade, and it's just as fitting that the East India Company would see the end of the 18th century with a ban on that very same opium trade. The final 58 years of the Company's existence would, however, have a lot more brewing than a hot cup of tea.

Chapter 3 – The Company's Third Century: The EIC's Military Exploits, Indian Nationalism, Racial and Religious Ideologies, and the Dissolution of the EIC

The EIC's Army in the 19th Century

As we saw in the earlier chapter, the East India Company's centers all had their own armies. In the beginning, all three of them—the armies of Bengal, Madras, and Bombay—would contain more than just British officers. Other Europeans and even some native Indians would occasionally rise to the rank of officer during their service. But in 1785, the Company issued a set of military reforms that prohibited anyone other than British soldiers from becoming officers. They did, however, still recruit native Indians, who would come to be known as sepoys.

By the first quarter of the 19th century, the Company's combined forces were probably the largest army in the world at the time, numbering well over 280,000 men. The vast majority of these men were sepoys, outnumbering the British troops almost ten to one. Interestingly, the British officers also far outnumbered the British civilians in the Company-owned lands of India.

The Company's army had a huge number of disadvantages, both when compared to the regular British troops as well as the local armies from the countries the EIC bordered. For example, there was a lot of division within the army. The Indians and the British officers didn't take too kindly to one another, and neither did the British officers from Britain to those of the Company. In addition, whenever we say "the Company's army," we have to keep in mind that we're discussing three separate armies from three very different trading centers. The soldiers from Bombay were not bred or trained in the same way as those from Bengal, for instance, or even those from Madras. This distinction between the three regiments brought about jealousy, envy, and even confusion on the battlefield. Other disadvantages included the lack of a proper cavalry and an even more significant lack of properly trained officers. Unlike other armies at the time, the soldiers of the Company were promoted based on their seniority, not their actual warfare skills.

With all of these issues in mind, anyone would think that the Company's army would fall apart and that they would be overtaken by a local Indian prince or a foreign trade rival with a semi-competent army. But precisely the opposite happened. As early as the 1760s, the Company's military had to face powerful local foes, such as the ruler of the Kingdom of Mysore, Hyder Ali, and, especially, his son, Tipu Sultan. Hyder would claim impressive victories over the British during two of the Anglo-Mysore Wars, the first waged between 1767 and 1769, and the second taking place between 1780 and 1784, with Hyder dying in 1782. After his death and Tipu's ascension, the British, led by Lord Cornwallis, would ally themselves with the Hyderabad State and the Maratha Empire and strike hard at the Mysore ruler. The Third Anglo-Mysore War ended in 1792 with the Treaty of Seringapatam. This treaty saw a now-humiliated Tipu Sultan surrender half of his territory and his two sons to Lord Cornwallis and pay a huge indemnity to the Company. But Mysore would see one more war, lasting from 1798 to 1799, and this time the Company's troops, led by Richard Wellesley, utterly crushed their Muslim rivals. Tipu Sultan was killed at one of the Seringapatam gates during the Siege of Seringapatam, and the vast majority of what was left of his land was annexed by the Company.

Though these victories came about at the end of the 18th century, they are an important precursor to the Company's policies in the early 1800s. Their next campaign would pit them against their former allies, the Marathas. Throughout the 1700s, the power of the Mughal Empire waned, which gave the Marathas an opportunity to expand and acquire new lands. With Wellesley now serving as the governor-general, the British clashed with the leader of the Maratha Empire in 1802. Two officers, Commander-in-Chief Gerard Lake and Arthur Wellesley (Richard's younger brother and the 1st Duke of Wellington), had achieved exceptional military successes that resulted in the annexation of large portions of Maratha lands to the Company. Armed with this military experience, Arthur Wellesley would later defeat Napoleon and earn himself the title of Duke of Wellington.

The last real challenge among the Indian territories that the Company had to face were the Sikhs in Punjab. Under the leadership of Ranjit Singh, and after the capture of the city of Lahore in 1799, the Sikhs would become a massive force that would come to rival the EIC's military. But after Ranjit Singh's death in 1839, the Sikhs were disunited, and the Company sought to use this opportunity to attack. During the First Anglo-Sikh War, which lasted from December 1845 to March 1846, the Company achieved victory, but their overall performance was less than stellar. The military was disjointed, leading wars on several separate fronts, and the biggest reason why the fighting ultimately ended in the favor of the Company was the disunity of the Sikh commanders and their defection to the British. At the end of the war, per the Treaty of Lahore, Ranjit Singh's underage son, Duleep Singh, would remain the ruler of the Sikh, but he would lose a lot of the Punjab territory. In 1848 and early 1849, the Company and the Sikh would fight their final war, the Second Anglo-Sikh War, which resulted in the decisive victory of the British and the complete and utter annexation of Punjab. Brothers John and Henry Lawrence would become the administrators of Punjab; this is an important historical footnote because it's thanks to their devotion to religion and their stance toward the locals that would shape how the British saw the Indians. In other words, the best examples of EIC's colonialism and racism would stem from the Lawrence brother's activities in the Company.

The Indian subcontinent wasn't the only area where the Company expanded territorially. For example, in 1795, they took control of Malacca, a settlement in the southeast of the Malay Peninsula, from the Dutch. They held Malacca until roughly 1818 when they returned it to the Dutch, only to gain it once more in 1824 in exchange for an old Sumatran pepper port called Bencoolen. North of the Malay coast, the British would fight Burma in two wars. After the treaties of 1826 and 1852, the Burmese lost vast swathes of territories to the Company, including the provinces of Arakan, Tenasserim, Lower Burma (known as Pegu), and, in 1885, Upper Burma. Surprisingly, the Company even had control over the island of Saint Helena during Napoleon Bonaparte's exile. In fact, during his entire "stay" on the island, from 1815 to 1821, Napoleon was effectively the prisoner of the East India Company.

Malacca wasn't the first Malay settlement that the EIC held. That honor goes to the settlement on Penang Island in 1786. The third and final settlement in Southeast Asia was founded by a company officer named Thomas Stamford Raffles. This settlement was at the very tip of the Malay Peninsula, and Raffles called it Singapore, a town that would become an economic powerhouse a few centuries later. Together, these three spots, collectively called the Straits Settlements (after the Malacca Strait), became the Company's fourth official presidency. On a darker note, they would more often than not serve as penal colonies for Indian convicts. However, Malacca already had a decently sized Indian community, as well as a large number of Chinese citizens. The Chinese would move south to trade at first, but when tin was discovered in the 1840s, they began to flock in even greater numbers in order to mine it. Even in its early days, Singapore and its nearest "neighbors" had an exceptionally diverse population.

A sepoy from the Madras army, unknown artist, 1835[v]

https://commons.wikimedia.org/wiki/File:Sepoy,_Madras_Army,_1835.jpg

Racial and Religious Ideologies

Interestingly, the question of the English Church in the EIC's territories wasn't a particularly hot-topic issue during the early days of the Company. While it is true that the British people had wanted churches and Christian missions since the late 1690s, the first actual efforts to send any type of missions came about a whole century later. Some experts trace it to the publication of William Carey's book *An Enquiry into the Obligations of Christians to Use Means for the Conversion of the Heathens* in 1792. As a Baptist missionary, Carey had likened Britain (and by extension the EIC) as a pillar of Christianity whose mission was to convert as many "barbarous heathens" as possible.

While the Company was young, it carried on the tradition of many Middle-Eastern and Indian rulers of the past by becoming a patron of the local adherents of Hinduism or Islam. As far back as antiquity, early Mesopotamian rulers would often do the same. In fact, allowing for different religions to continue their preaching is a prudent political move; not only does it prevent rebellions from sprouting out of nowhere, but it also keeps the locals satisfied and, more importantly, loyal to the new regime.

Britain itself had lots of internal religious issues. While the Church of England had been the official religion of the kingdom since the 1530s, dissenters such as Baptists, Methodists, and Presbyterians also preached openly. The political parties at the time (the Whigs and the Tories) had major disagreements in regard to these other Christian denominations. The Whigs tolerated then, whereas the Tories were their staunch opponents. It didn't help matters that a new Evangelical movement was taking the kingdom by storm. So, at least at the beginning of the 19th century, it didn't seem likely that the Church would overwhelm the Muslim and Hindu areas under the EIC's control. In fact, they even tried to stave off any missions to the Indian subcontinent, fearing that conversions and Christian missions would cause rebellions. More importantly, building and maintaining churches were expensive endeavors, something that wasn't particularly profitable to anyone in the Company.

Soon enough, however, that would change. The Company's treatment of Christian missionaries (of all denominations) would cause several strong religious figures to respond fervently, including two of the people most responsible for the active Christian efforts in the region. The first was Charles Grant, a late 18th-century

Evangelical Anglican author who called Hindus and Muslims "depraved" in his works and claimed that they did this out of ignorance of Christ and Christian ways. The other important figure was William Wilberforce, the same man who helped end the British slave trade in 1807 and championed the abolition of slavery throughout the British Empire. Wilberforce and Grant prepared a document that would later become the famous pious clause, which required the EIC to finance and actively send out Christian missionaries. The clause was an essential part of the new EIC charter when 1813 rolled around, the same year when the Anglican Indian Church was established.

Wilberforce died in 1833, which was an important year for Christian missionaries in India. During this year, a new charter was issued, lifting any and all restrictions on Christian missionaries who wanted to spread the word of God in the EIC's territories. One such restriction, as made clear by the 1813 charter, was that a missionary had to get a license from the Company. With this move, there was clearly a shift in the EIC's policies toward religion. But interestingly, this shift went side by side with the Company's views on race.

Some supporters of Grant and Wilberforce, such as the Anglican Reverend Claudius Buchanan, claimed that it was England's duty to civilize Indians through religion. The early 19th century seemed to intertwine the idea of foreigners being non-Christian to the racial superiority of the English. Though there were racial tensions before these Christian efforts at the beginning of the 1800s, it was this century that would amp them up to eleven. Not only did the Company's men treat the locals like lesser beings, but the locals also began to unite to forge a common identity that despised the conquering white lords. All of these events would be the seeds of the most turbulent period in the Company's history, one that would lead to its downfall.

Indian Nationalism and Rebellion

The EIC had been encroaching on the territories of Indian states for centuries, but it would only be through a series of unfair and British-centric reforms that it would escalate into a full-blown rebellion.

Lords, such as Lord William Bentinck, a governor-general during the late 1820s and early 1830s, wanted to impose British values onto the local populace by, for example, abolishing the practice of sati. Among the Hindus of EIC-contemporary India, a widow would sometimes sacrifice herself by burning atop her late husband's funeral pyre. Though hundreds of widows practiced sati on a yearly basis at the time, it wasn't that common, at least when compared to other Hindu practices. Nevertheless, that didn't stop Bentinck and his supporters from abolishing it in 1829 and declaring it as an example of the "decadent" Hindu system. Works of local Indian intellectuals, such as Ram Mohan Roy, would help the British pursue their goals of secularization and "Britishization" of the Indian lands. Then there were Parliament members, such as Thomas Babington Macaulay, who argued that the British had a mission to civilize Indian lands and that the Company, even without having a trade monopoly, should govern these territories independently of the UK. According to Macaulay and his supporters, the Company couldn't finance the education of the local Indians, and the few that did get higher education and/or a position within the EIC (though those were rare for the non-British) would serve as interpreters between the Company and the massive local populace.

"Civilizing" Indians and abolishing sati were just two of several ways in which the British sought to assert their dominance in the region. By the 1830s, for example, Persian was almost exclusively replaced in elementary schools by English. In addition, there was a massive public campaign against local gang members called the *thagi*, who strangled rich travelers (interestingly, this is where the English word "thug" originated from). However, these changes did not originally impact Indians on a wide scale. Rather, the effects were felt locally, and they didn't demand a lot of attention by Indian rulers or even the common folk.

However, thanks to the efforts of the EIC's London administrator James Mill and later his son, the famed philosopher and classical liberal John Stuart Mill, the British would take a more active role in subjugating the Indians. According to contemporary thinkers, the Indian civilization had been in a decline for decades, if not centuries, and the British were the best people to provide them with a proper cultural upbringing. This, of course, was a sentiment that the Indians seriously disagreed with over the course of the next few decades.

The EIC had, paradoxically, been in a steep decline during the years before the Indian nationalist rebellion that was to come. The British Parliament had ended its monopoly on trade with India in 1813 and with China in 1833, which gave free traders a chance to expand and out-earn the Company's merchants. In addition, the EIC was under heavy scrutiny, and the English lords were waiting for the perfect opportunity to strip them of their power. There was a growing sentiment that the Crown should take direct charge of the Company and cripple their independent endeavors on the subcontinent. It's quite the historical paradox that the British government would actively work against one of its richest assets, especially during the time that, despite all of its setbacks, the Company was in a decent condition. They controlled more land than they ever did before, and trade, despite its new limitations, was still going strong.

However, the "swinging" at the Company didn't just come from above. There was also a growing resentment among the local Indians, people who did not share a common heritage (let's remember that this was a period of warring independent countries with different religious, political, and social views) but whose disdain of the British united them to help forge what would become a uniform Indian identity. The biggest blow to the locals, and the first in the line of sweeping reforms that would lead to rebellion, was the introduction of uniform coinage in 1835. Up until then, most Indians used a wide variety of coins made from different metals, but their defining characteristic had been that they had been issued in the name of Shah Allam II, a Mughal emperor who had been dead since 1806. When the Company felt sufficiently secure in coining their own mint, thanks to the efforts of Bentinck's successor, Sir Charles Metcalfe, they did so with the portrait of the active British monarch, King William IV (1765-1837). Not only did this cement the notion that the British king was the ruler of all the Indian lands, but it also created the conditions for a uniform India, a single, unified country. Building railroads and connecting the many parts of this new "country" in the early 1850s only further confirmed that.

Naturally, there were multiple small rebellions in the long history of the EIC. However, the Company dealt with these locally, treating them as little more than outbreaks of civil disobedience. It was the Indian rebellion of 1857 that shook the EIC to its core. In just one turbulent year, Southeast Asia would be rocked by spectacular, bloody battles and catastrophic defeats, but it would also see the end of the East India Company and the definite rise of the United Kingdom as the dominant imperial force in the known world.

The rebellion was sparked on May 10th by a group of unsatisfied sepoys from Meerut, a town roughly forty miles northeast of Delhi. Just a day before, the local British officers sentenced 85 other sepoys to ten years of imprisonment because they refused to use cartridges for the new Enfield rifle. These cartridges were thought to be greased with pig and cow fat, which later turned out not to be true. It was an effective cause to start a wide-scale rebellion, though; cows are sacred animals to the Hindu religion, and the Muslims consider using any product that comes from a pig to be *haram*, i.e., forbidden. With this single move, the British officers gave the sepoys more than enough reason to attack. However, the Enfield incident was merely the boiling point. The Indian troops had been receiving lower wages for decades now, and some of them hadn't been paid at all in years. In addition, there were officers among the British Army that proselytized Christian beliefs, and many local troops started converting. There were also new regulations that forced Indian soldiers to fight in any area of the Company, regardless of how far it was from their native town.

Most of the soldiers that started the rebellion were native to the state of Awadh, which became independent after the collapse of the Mughal Empire but was annexed by Governor-General James Broun-Ramsay, also known as Lord Dalhousie, in 1856. Dalhousie had already annexed a great number of Indian states by this point, invoking the so-called Doctrine of Lapse from the late 1840s. According to this doctrine, if there was no legitimate male heir to an Indian principality, that territory was treated as a "lapse" state; therefore, it was the duty of the EIC to take it over.

Because of Awadh's annexation, new landholding and revenue laws were introduced. The local landowners, or *Taluqdars*, largely lost their rights to collect revenue or were faced with excruciating revenue demands, while the peasants suffered the brunt of these reforms. In other words, both the Indian officers and the underclasses had more than enough reason to unite against a common enemy and were more than willing to join the rebels.

The native Indians scored their first major victory when they took over Delhi and declared the aging Bahadur Shah as the new Mughal emperor, their leader in name only. In practice, three rebel leaders were much more prominent. These leaders were Nana Sahib, who was the adopted son of Baji Rao II, the last peshwa (prime minister) of the state of Maratha; Tantia Tope, who was the son of a Maratha courtier; and Lakshmibai, also known as the Rani (queen) of Jhansi. Soon enough, most of the northern EIC territories were under the control of the rebels.

The EIC was caught off-guard by this rebellion, so they acted quickly. Their first order of business was to recapture Delhi, which they held under siege for six long days in September until they finally took it. Bahadur Shah was exiled to Burma, and his sons were all executed. This was one of the biggest victories of the Company during the rebellion, but it wasn't easy to rally the troops. In fact, it was thanks to the massacre at Cawnpore in June of 1857 that the British finally began to take action against the rebels. During the EIC era, the city of Cawnpore (modern-day Kanpur) was an important garrison, complete with barracks. The forces of Nana Sahib and Tantia Tope besieged the city and held the British hostage for several weeks. Ultimately, they agreed to let them go once the British surrendered, but for reasons that are still unknown to modern historians, the Indians proceeded to massacre most of the EIC's men, women, children, and the elderly. The remaining 200 or so people were brought back to the city and captured, only to be executed later. A few British captives managed to escape.

The massacre at Cawnpore, known as the Bibighar massacre, was a devastating event, but it was also used as a reason to rally the troops against the Indians. The vengeance of the British was brutal; thanks to the newly-issued Act XIV (shortly after the Siege of Cawnpore), the EIC had the full legal right to prosecute and sentence any Indian they deemed to be collaborating with the rebels. The governor-general at the time, Lord Charles Canning, actually issued a revised set of guidelines for Act XIV on how to approach the sentencing, guidelines that the British officers and troops almost universally reviled, giving the governor-general the nickname "Clemency Canning." The EIC would score a few more victories and wage a few more battles that became legendary in the history of Britain, including the famed Siege of Lucknow. The Lucknow Residency became a refuge for the British once the rebellion actually reached Lucknow on July 1st, 1857. However, despite being besieged on numerous sides, the British held the line until November 27th when the Indian forces lifted the siege.

Late 1857 and early 1858 saw the crushing of the rebellion. Lakshmibai was fighting the EIC's forces in her native state of Jhansi, which was, just like Awadh, annexed by Lord Dalhousie before the rebellion. Despite losing key battles, the queen managed to escape and join Tantia Tope in a combined effort to invade the city of Gwalior. On June 17th, 1858, Lakshmibai died in battle, and

Tantia Tope was betrayed and killed in April the next year. The only rebel leader to survive was Nana Sahib, who fled and was never heard from again. The rebellion was officially declared to have ended on November 1st, 1858, but the hostilities did not end until October 1859 when the British crushed the remaining rebels in the Gujarat region.

Portrait of Ram Mohan Roy, unknown artist, 1820[vi]

https://commons.wikimedia.org/wiki/File:Bust_portrait_of_the_Hindu_reformer_Ram_Moh an_Roy.jpg

The End of the Company

The EIC would not finish the war as an independent entity, however. For years, Parliament had been meddling in the Company's affairs, taking a more active role as an overseer. The Company did manage to renew its charter in 1853, but this time, there was no twenty-year period before the next renewal, as was the custom. As soon as the rebellion took place, Parliament saw an opportunity to finally take control of the Company and place it directly under the influence of the government. On August 2nd, 1858, Parliament issued the Government of India Act, which demanded that the Company's officials transfer all of their power to the Crown. Historically speaking, this date marks the official end of the East India Company. However, the Company's officials continued their work, and the shareholders continued to get a dividend from the EIC's trade revenues. It wouldn't be until June 1874 that these dividends would be fully redeemed, the proprietors reimbursed, and the Company's books officially closed. Though the Company ceased to be an independent actor in 1858, it was finally put to rest in 1874, ushering in the age of the British Raj in India that would last until 1947.

The Double Mohur with the depiction of King William IV, 1835[vii]

https://commons.wikimedia.org/wiki/File:India_1835_2_Mohurs.jpg

Chapter 4 – Effects of the EIC: Changes in the British Society, Impact on Local People Groups, and Growth of the British Empire

The Relationship of the Indians and the EIC

During its infancy, the East India Company didn't have a lot of impact on local or global politics. It had been one of many different overseas enterprises that the European powers controlled, and as was the case with all of them, it was extremely volatile and ready to snap at any moment. However, as its power grew, the effects of the Company's actions were felt across both Europe and Asia.

As it grew, the Company became a dominant political player in the Indian subcontinent. Local princes and minor political players tolerated the Company's merchants at first, treating them as a potential "asset" that paid tributes as much as any vassal might. But near the end of the 18th century, as the Company gradually shifted its focus from merchants to rulers, the political landscape of India had drastically changed. The once-mighty Mughal Empire who had dominated the region was reduced to a fraction of its former territory, with other states (like Awadh) emerging; needless to say, the Company's growth and influence helped these new states rise to power. However, the governor-general and the Board of Directors actually held enough power and sway to overthrow entire governments and install their own puppet rulers. Parallels can be drawn between the events of the decline of the Roman Empire and the situation in India during the existence of the East India Company; the gradual fall of the Mughal Empire, the rise of minor local powers, and the influence a group of outsider upstarts (i.e., the British) had over everyone is not unlike the expanding growth of the Gothic kingdoms and the Celts and Anglo-Saxons in Britain as the Roman state deteriorated further and further. In fact, just as there were Roman citizens who recognized the sovereignty and power of early Gothic rulers and some Celtic kings, there were powerful Indian rulers who had no problem being in the hands of the East India Company. Or rather, they had no real choice in the matter considering the extravagant debts they would owe to the British. This development had made the local Indian populace, princes and peasants alike, resent the Company way before there were even hints of a wide-scale rebellion.

It goes without saying that the British were a major factor in the ruination of the Indian states, but it would be disingenuous to claim that the Indians were completely innocent in all of it. Since the earliest days of the Company, the local princes would fight for power, and the Mughal Empire was ready to do anything to maintain their stranglehold. In fact, during the Company's formative years, Indian rulers would regularly employ their services in order to overthrow a different ruler or conquer a region. Political intrigue was powerful on the Indian subcontinent way before the English even set foot on its shores. But it's that same intrigue that helped the Company rise and become the de facto master of the Indian states.

The Company at Home

Of course, the Indians weren't the only ones who would come to despites the EIC. As it grew and prospered, the Company had made enemies back in Britain as well. Because of its policy to hire young men from all walks of life, as it held the possibility that lower-class men would gain the opportunity to grow as rich and powerful as the prominent lords in Britain, Parliament sought out every opportunity to nip the Company in the bud. Moreover, Parliament officials tended to owe a lot of money to the EIC, though, paradoxically, quite a few of them were actually its investors and shareholders. The Company's downfall could have possibly ended the lucrative endeavors of some lords, but it would have several important benefits to the British ruling class. First off, their debts would be erased or otherwise revised to the lords' benefits. Next, they would get to control the wealthy trade that the Company had a monopoly over or, at the very least, send their own agents as competition. Finally, they would secure their own position in society and not allow any low-born nobodies to climb to the top.

Interestingly, as racist and segregationist as the British were to the native Indians during the Company's later years, they were no less bigoted toward their fellow Englishmen who came to find success and wealth in the Company. The pejorative term "nabob" became exceptionally popular in those days. It was a corruption of the Urdu word nawab (meaning prince, usually a prince subordinate to the Mughal Empire), and it came into prominence as early as 1612 as a way to distinguish a person who acquired a suspicious amount of wealth in a short amount of time. Once nabobs started buying up seats in Parliament, the popular opinion of them deteriorated further, and they were mocked publicly by all social classes. They would frequently purchase old, splendid houses in counties like Berkshire, Wiltshire, Hertfordshire, and Essex and then proceed to either repair or expand them. More often than not, these homes would be filled with riches and objects from Indian states, but it wasn't uncommon to see Chinese wallpaper and other such items displayed. Most of the time, these objects were purchased simply due to the whims of the nabobs, but it wasn't uncommon for the British who lived and worked in the EIC territories their whole lives to develop affections toward the cultures there. Needless to say, that didn't exactly help their social status and the public opinion of them back in Britain.

Chapter 5 – Notable Individuals of the EIC Era

There's a reason this chapter has the title that it has; both England and the Indian states had been home to exceptional individuals who had a strong impact on the course of the Company's history, as well as history in general. However, we won't delve into the contemporary English monarchs, such as Queens Elizabeth I and Victoria or Kings Charles II or William of Orange, nor will we get into what Oliver Cromwell did during the "Republic era." The reason behind this decision is that there's already a plethora of information on every single one of them out there. This chapter will instead focus on the local rulers from the surrounding Hindu and Muslim states, as well as the officials of the Company and even a few everyday individuals that helped to shape the future of India. These individuals are listed in alphabetical order according to their surname, where applicable.

Aurangzeb

Ruling for an impressive period of 49 years from July 31st, 1658, to March 3rd, 1707, Aurangzeb was by far the most powerful and influential Mughal emperor in history. As a major patron of Islam, he was one of the first rulers to successfully implement Sharia law throughout his land, as well as one of the wealthiest men at the time (though he would not live an extravagant life and would often use his own wealth to build and repair mosques throughout the subcontinent). While he wasn't particularly fond of non-Muslim religions, he was still a patron of the local Hindu people and had employed a great number of Hindu scholars and officials at his court.

During his reign, the East India Company was still far from being an established force. The First Anglo-Mughal War initiated by Josiah Child saw a humiliating defeat of the British. In 1695, five years after the war had ended, a British pirate called Henry Avery captured one of Aurangzeb's convoys in the Indian Ocean, looting the ships and murdering the crews. It was the greatest pirate raid in known history at the time, and Aurangzeb didn't take the news well. At first, he wanted to crush the British entirely and to effectively scrub them from the subcontinent, but ultimately, the Company settled with a substantial sum of money, an estimated 600,000 pounds. That didn't stop Aurangzeb from expressing his rage, however, considering that he shut down four EIC factories and imprisoned their workers in the process. In order to quell the emperor's rage, the Company issued a bounty for Avery's capture and initiated one of the biggest manhunts of the 17th century. Avery, however, was never brought to justice for what he did.

During Aurangzeb's reign, the Mughal Empire became wealthier and more prosperous than contemporary Qing China, and his estimated wealth dwarfed every European ruler at the time. Other than the very south of the subcontinent, the entire modern territory of India came to be under his direct rule. After his death, the Mughals would suffer a slow but substantial decline, which the EIC would capitalize on throughout the centuries.

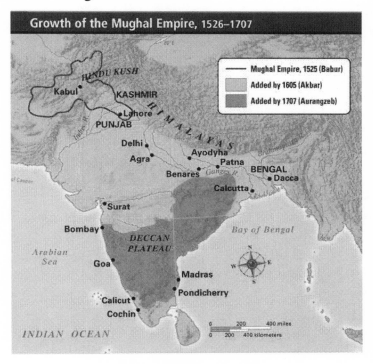

The Mughal Empire at its peak[viii]

Santosh.mbahrm, CC BY-SA 3.0 <https://creativecommons.org/licenses/by-sa/3.0>, via Wikimedia Commons https://commons.wikimedia.org/wiki/File:Mughal-empire-map.jpg

Lakshmibai

One of the three figureheads of the 1857 Rebellion, the fourteen-year-old Manikarnika Tambe would come to be the wife of Gangadhar Newalkar, the last maharaja (a title that means "great king") of an independent Jhansi state. Manikarnika would be named Lakshmibai (or Laxmi Bai) after their marriage to honor the Hindu goddess of wealth and prosperity, Lakshmi.

During the reign of her husband, Jhansi was a somewhat peaceful state. Sadly, the pair's only son, Damodar Rao, would die four months after being born, so they decided to adopt the maharaja's nephew, Anand Rao, and raise him as an heir. After the maharaja's death in 1853, Lakshmibai became the queen regent, ruling until Anand Rao came of age. However, since Anand wasn't a direct heir of Gangadhar Newalkar, Lord Dalhousie seized the opportunity and invaded Jhansi, and in 1854, Lakshmibai was forced to depart her country, an act she would work hard to avenge.

Lakshmibai was not like other Indian women of the period. As a youth, she was a fencer, a wrestler, an avid horse rider, and an independent-minded politician. Interestingly, she didn't initially intend to rebel. In June 1857, the Indian Bengali mutineers sacked the state's capital, which was also named Jhansi, and Lakshmibai took control of the region once again, but she wanted to rule the country in the name of the British, petitioning them for assistance. Up until January of 1858, all the minor invasions by local claimants to the throne of Jhansi were fended off by Lakshmibai, and the local support for her grew. Once the British arrived to take direct control of Jhansi in March of the same year, Lakshmibai fortified the city and refused to surrender. However, the overwhelming forces of the Company, led in combat by Field Marshal Hugh Rose, ultimately won. Lakshmibai and her son fled the city, which was promptly sacked and looted for days.

Lakshmibai joined Tantia Tope's forces, and together they invaded the state of Gwalior and laid siege to its namesake capital. She was supposedly killed in battle on June 17th by one of the 8th King's Royal Irish Hussars at the village of Kotah-ki-Serai just outside of Gwalior. Her adopted son fled to the woods, surrendering to the British after he settled in the city of Indore.

Painting of Rani Lakshmibai, unknown artist, 1947[ix]

https://commons.wikimedia.org/wiki/File:Rani_Lakshmibai_from_a_painting.jpg

Robert Clive

The famed "Clive of India" is possibly one of the best-known examples of why working for the EIC was as rewarding as it was damaging. A prominent military commander and the first governor of the EIC, Clive repeatedly crushed the efforts of the Indian princes and established the Company as a force to be reckoned with. During his tenure in the East India Company, Clive managed to overthrow the Bengal prince, effectively seizing control of the wealthiest province at the time. In addition, he worked hard on suppressing the French from controlling the Indian trade, adopting their system of ruling the local states through puppet governments. His military exploits and countless victories earned him millions of pounds, and he had even bought himself a seat in Parliament. But his methods were routinely criticized by his contemporaries. Clive was known to raise taxes and reduce yearly earnings in order to rein in spending. In addition, forced cultivations of crops under his rule led to some of the worst famines that the Indian subcontinent has ever witnessed. Perplexingly, though not unexpectedly, Clive would vehemently defend his position in front of the other lords, citing how the nabobs of Britain did more good than harm and claiming that the princes of the Indian states were no better than tyrants.

Clive died on November 22nd, 1774, at the age of 49. Considering that he had joined the Company in 1744 and retired around 1768, his 24-year tenure is nothing short of impressive. During this time, he rose to prominence from a petty assistant to one of the greatest governors the East India Company had fostered.

Warren Hastings

The first proper governor-general of India was Warren Hastings, who came from a poor, albeit aristocratic, family. Born in 1732, he joined the EIC when he turned eighteen. Interestingly, despite his noteworthy efforts during the retaking of Calcutta in 1757 and his tenure as the British resident (an ambassador of sorts) in Murshidabad, the capital of Bengal, Hastings wanted to approach the Indians in a more moderate way than his peers. Interestingly, he resigned from the Company twice. During the period of his first resignation (1764 to 1769), he returned to England and began to spend copious amounts of money. Having accrued outstanding debts, he saw his return to the Company as the quickest way to earn more money. Upon his arrival, he was appointed the governor of Bengal, a position he held until 1773 when the Regulating Act subsumed the presidencies of Madras and Bombay under that of Bengal. At that point, he was elevated to the position of governor-general, and he held dominion over the Company until his second resignation in 1785. Upon his return, Hastings was impeached in the House of Commons. The members of Parliament had accused him of various crimes, and the long, drawn-out trial would supposedly cost Hastings an incredible 70,000 pounds overall. He was ultimately acquitted of all charges on April 24th, 1795, and he passed away in 1818 at the ripe age of 85. To this day, Hastings is remembered as one of the few people at the very top of the East India Company who saw the value of learning about the various cultures of India and treating the Indians with the respect that any British citizen deserved.

Portrait of Warren Hastings by Tilly Kettle, circa 1772[x]

https://commons.wikimedia.org/wiki/File:Warren_Hastings_by_Tilly_Kettle.jpg

Fanny Parkes

Frances Susanna Archer, later known as Fanny Parkes later, was a wife of an East India Company writer, Charles Crawford Parkes, and an avid writer herself; during her life in India between 1822 and 1846, she had learned Persian, Hindustani, and Urdu and had traveled throughout the country on horseback, writing down her impressions of the country and its people from the wealthiest to the neediest. Her memoir, called *Wanderings of a Pilgrim in Search of the Picturesque*, included select Indian proverbs translated to English, as well as a glossary of terms, and it is an invaluable piece of history as a firsthand account of contemporary India during the EIC's dominion.

Parkes was one of the first women, and indeed one of the first British in general, to publicly condemn some of the Hindu practices that harmed women, like sati. In addition, she protested the proposed plan to sell away the Taj Mahal, a noteworthy historical landmark that stands to this day, and she frequently spoke out against the officials who would present the local Indians and their customs in an unfavorable light.

Ram Mohan Roy

Similar to Parkes, one famed Indian scholar and raja (a title equivalent to a king) would work hard to abolish the practices that harmed women and children, including sati, arranged child marriage, polygamy, the caste system, and the lack of property inheritance rights for Indian women. That man was the acclaimed Ram Mohan Roy, famous for his various social reforms, as well as his monotheistic reformist movement known as Brahmo Sabha (which would later become Brahmo Samaj).

While employed by the EIC, Roy started work on his religious reforms, and many different religions, most notably Christianity, influenced his new doctrine. He was an advocate of maintaining a secular, scholarly India and worked hard in strengthening local education. He was the founder of the Anglo-Hindu school and the Vedanta College and helped set up Calcutta's Hindu College. Within Vedanta, he insisted that a Western educational style be implemented and that his new religious doctrine was mandatory. Because of his influence, Mughal Emperor Akbar Shah II bestowed upon him the title of raja to the court of British King William IV in 1830. Now a celebrity of sorts in both India and the UK, Roy traveled to Britain, where he would die in 1833 of meningitis. Both nations remember Roy fondly as someone who found that fine line between the East and the West and used it to improve the educational, religious, and legal systems of the Indians while staying loyal to the Company.

Nana Sahib

Another major name in the 1857 Rebellion was Nana Sahib (sometimes called Saheb). He was born in 1824 and was adopted three years later by Baji Rao II, an exiled former Maratha peshwa, who didn't have any of his own children. During his youth, Nana would befriend both Lakshmibai and Tantia Tope, who was also his fencing master.

Since Baji Rao died without issue, Nana Sahib was meant to inherit Baji Rao's EIC-provided pension of 80,000 pounds a year. However, it was during this time that Lord Dalhousie was implementing the Doctrine of Lapse to conquer various states. Much like with Lakshmibai's son, Nana wasn't able to inherit the throne of Maratha since he wasn't a blood relative to Baji Rao. And, once again similarly to Lakshmibai, Nana Sahib was originally a supporter of the Company in the early days of the rebellion, despite the slight regarding his annual pension. It would be on June 6th, 1857, that Nana would officially declare his support for the rebel cause and marched on the city of Cawnpore. He, along nearly 15,000 troops, laid siege to the city for twenty days until the British decided to surrender, provided they were given a safe passage out via the river dock called Satichaura Ghat. Whatever happened next is enshrouded in mystery and speculation, but the Indians fired on the British, and the event became forever known as the Satichaura Ghat massacre, with the aforementioned Bibighar massacre occurring almost three weeks later.

Nana Sahib would hold out against the British until the recapture of Cawnpore on July 19th, 1857, but he was never imprisoned or killed. Some speculate that he fled to Nepal or Sihor, a town in Gujarat, but accounts differ and often contain lots of contradictions.

As a rebel leader, Nana Sahib was an inspiration to thousands of people and is hailed as a national hero today. He even showed a level of mercy toward his prisoners, adamantly refusing to execute or torture women and children even after being pressured to issue the order. The fact that he was never captured only added to his heroic status in later years, and most people today associate the rebellion with him as the figurehead.

Nana Sahib, from Illustrated London News, 1857[xi]

https://commons.wikimedia.org/wiki/File:%22Nana_Sahib%22_(Dhundu_Pant).jpg

Ranjit Singh

A teenage prodigy general, a devout Sikh with imperial aspirations, a man of many wives and sons and twice as many mistresses, and an adorer of alcohol, Ranjit Singh was possibly one of the most prominent figures in India during the existence of the EIC, and his exploits rivaled those of other famed historical figureheads, such as Emperor Aurangzeb.

As an infant, Singh contracted smallpox, which left him with a scarred face and the loss of sight in his left eye. Though not formally schooled and could only write using the Gurmukhi alphabet, he was a proficient horse rider, musketeer, and martial artist. His childhood was quite eventful; at the age of twelve, his father died, making Singh the heir of his estate, whose care was left to his mother, Raj Kaur. Then at age thirteen, an attempt was made on his life, which he survived; he even managed to kill his assassin. Two years later, he would marry his first wife, Mehtab Kaur, but the marriage wasn't fruitful since Mehtab held a grudge against Singh's family. Namely, Singh's father had killed her father, and the marriage had been prearranged to bring peace between their two *misls* (a *misl* was a sovereign state in the 18th-century Sikh confederacy, and during Singh's time, these states were extremely disunited and warred frequently). It was also during these years that he began drinking, becoming somewhat of an alcoholic in his later life. But it was at the age of seventeen, one year before reaching adulthood and before his mother passed away, that Singh really became a prominent name in contemporary Sikh society. It was then that he successfully fended off the army of Shah Zaman, an Afghan Muslim leader of the Ahmad Shah Abdali royal house. Merely two years later, he and his mother-in-law, Rani Sada Kaur, would attack and conquer Lahore, a region that was at the time controlled by the Bhangi Sikh sect. Declaring himself the maharaja of Punjab in 1801, Singh would go on to conquer most of northwestern India and establish a stable, strong Sikh Empire.

Interestingly, Ranjit Singh employed people of nearly all religious and ethnic backgrounds except for the British. But even more amusingly, he kept diplomatic relations with them and even cooperated with the Company in removing local hostile Islamic rulers. It was only after his death that the EIC would go after the

Sikhs, and his son and heir, Duleep Singh, was effectively made their vassal.

Charles Stuart

Perhaps no man had been as big of a supporter of Hinduism and the Indian culture during the East India Company's existence than Charles "Hindoo" Stuart. Born in Ireland, Stuart became a soldier of the Company in his teenage years, soon rising to the rank of major general. However, he was to be best known for his open and unabashed love for the Hindu culture. For example, he would bathe in the Ganges River every morning and had a collection of Hindu icons and statues of their deities. Soon enough, he even began to wear Indian garb and was notorious for his sepoy forces who did not conform to their native traditions (such as sporting the wrong kind of mustaches or not wearing brightly colored caste marks). Most amusingly, he expressed his opinions on the Hindu women's dress code and why it was superior to European women's clothing in a published series of letters with a curiously short title, *The Ladies Monitor, Being A Series of Letters First published in Bengal on the Subject of Female Apparel Tending to Favour a regulated adoption of Indian Costume And a rejection of Superfluous Vesture By the Ladies of this country With Incidental remarks on Hindoo Beauty, Whale-Bone Stays, Iron Busks, Indian Corsets, Man-Milliners, Idle Bachelors, Hair-Powder, Waiting Maids, And Footmen.*

Of course, the book of letters regarding the superior Indian garb was far from the only piece of writing Stuart composed on the topic of Hinduism and Indian culture. In fact, he wrote countless newspaper articles and full-length books arguing in favor of adopting Indian cultural norms in Britain. He was just as adamant in defending the culture against constant attacks from other Company officials, as well as critics from the outside, most commonly those from the British Parliament.

Tipu Sultan

The Kingdom of Mysore was ruled by the Wadiyar dynasty from 1399 to 1956, but for a brief period, two military commanders were in control, and during their reign, the kingdom flourished. The first of these two was Hyder Ali, the commander-in-chief of Maharaja Chamaraja Wodeyar IX. While the maharaja was still the rightful ruler, the control of the kingdom was effectively in Ali's hands. However, the second non-Wadiyar ruler of Mysore would not limit himself to being a mere commander-in-chief and would come to abolish the Wadiyar regime, declaring himself the padishah ("Great King") of the land. That man was Hyder Ali's son, Tipu Sultan.

Known as the man who perfected early rocketry and as a highly-educated and capable Islamic thinker, Tipu Sultan was one of the staunchest enemies of the East India Company. One of his first clashes with the British was at the Battle of Pollilur during the Second Anglo-Mysore War in 1780, where he crushed the forces of Lieutenant Colonel William Baillie using highly effective Mysorean rockets. His most noteworthy fights against the EIC would occur during the end of 1799 when he invaded the Kingdom of Travancore and initiated the Third Anglo-Mysore War. This small kingdom was an ally of the Company, and as Sultan's forces advanced, Maharaja Dharma Raja sought help from the EIC, and Lord Cornwallis responded. During the next three years, Sultan would achieve a few notable victories, but the alliance of the EIC, the Hyderabad State, and the Marathas kept inching closer to the Mysore capital. Tipu Sultan lost the war in the end, and his sons, as well as a vast area of his land, were now under direct Company control. Sultan himself would live to fight in the Fourth Anglo-Mysore War. Some sources claim that the French military advisors at his court advised retreat once the British breached the walls of the capital, but Sultan had refused to do so, staying defiant to the end. Upon his death, the Wadiyar dynasty had been restored, with Krishnaraja Wadiyar III being crowned as the new maharaja.

Tipu Sultan had a profound impact on the Mysore people. Thanks to his economic reforms, the daily wages in the kingdom were higher than anywhere else in the known world. Though he was known to occasionally persecute Christians, Hindus, and at times even other Muslims, he had employed people of all nationalities (save the British) at his court and had actively endowed and restored over 150 different Hindu temples. His revolutionary rocketry system had been carefully studied by the British after Mysore had been conquered and became one of the cornerstones of British rocket engineering. Due to his ferocity and skills, Sultan was dubbed the Tiger of Mysore.

Lord Cornwallis receiving Tipu Sultan's sons as hostages after his victory by Robert Home, circa 1793[xii]

https://commons.wikimedia.org/wiki/File:Surrender_of_Tipu_Sultan.jpg

Tantia Tope

A childhood friend of Nana Sahib, Tantia Tope would become his supporter during the rebellion, acting out of the town of Bithur. As a military commander, he was present during the Siege of Cawnpore and had fled the city once it was reconquered by the British. Alongside Nana Sahib's nephew Rao Sahib, Tope went to help

Lakshmibai escape Jhansi. United, the three took control of Gwalior and declared it a free kingdom in the name of Nana Sahib. Gwalior would soon fall as well, and both Tope and Rao Sahib fled, with Tope continuing his military exploits as a guerilla fighter. He would survive the dissolution of the East India Company but was captured and executed by hanging in April 1859.

Richard Wellesley

An Irish aristocrat at birth, Richard Wellesley was educated at some of the most elite schools in Britain, including both Eton and Harrow. In 1793, he acquired a membership on the Board of Control over Indian affairs, which slowly got him acquainted with the situation on the Indian subcontinent; a mere four years later, he became the governor-general of the Company. His first year in India would prove to be eventful, as it was the period when Tipu Sultan was forging an alliance with the French in order to reduce the influence of the Company. As early as February 1799, Wellesley's campaign against the Kingdom of Mysore was a success, though it was just the beginning of a string of effective military campaigns. His wars against the Maratha Empire would claim vast territories for the Company, utterly remove the French from the subcontinent, and add tens of millions of pounds in revenue to the Crown. In addition, he founded several institutions in India that would help educate future governors-general and other potential higher-ups of the Company. There's no doubt that Wellesley was instrumental in sowing the seeds of an imperial Britain thanks to his actions both on the battlefield and in the office.

Wellesley resigned from the EIC in 1805, but his political career didn't end in India. Four years later, he would become an ambassador to Spain and a foreign secretary not long after that, a position he held until 1812. He would also hold the office of lord lieutenant of Ireland twice, the first time from 1821 to 1828 and again from 1833 to 1835, which was the year when he finally retreated from public life altogether. He died in 1842 and was buried in Eton College Chapel.

Richard Wellesley's life was just as intriguing as his exploits in India and Europe. For instance, he had five wives, including the French actress Hyacinthe-Gabrielle Roland, who did not speak a word of English. His own multiple children had been scorned by most of Wellesley's extended family members and were collectively known as "The Parasites" for their unhealthy influence on their father. Furthermore, Wellesley was a fiery supporter of the Catholic emancipation. Since the establishment of the Church of England, the Catholics were prevented from several key social practices, including holding office. Thanks to the efforts of Wellesley's brother, Arthur, the 1st Duke of Wellington, the Roman Catholic Relief Act was passed in 1829, which incentivized Wellesley into returning as the lord lieutenant of Ireland several years later.

But most interestingly, Wellesley would suffer mysterious "black-outs" from time to time when he held public speeches, though he was known as an eloquent and mellifluous speaker. One such black-out happened in 1812 when he needed to give a speech to denounce the new government; this incident would follow him throughout his remaining years.

Portrait of Richard Wellesley, 1st Marquess Wellesley by Martin Archer Shee, circa 1832 xiii

William Wilberforce

William Wilberforce came from a wealthy family but was a sickly child with poor eyesight. During his early years, he had a propensity for playing cards, attending balls, and visiting the theater, which soon led to gambling and excessive drinking. In 1777, at the age of eighteen, Wilberforce inherited the wealth of his recently deceased grandfather and uncle, which made him disinterested in his studies but did not prevent him from acquiring both a bachelor's degree (in 1781) and a master's degree (in 1788). During these early days, he had developed an interest in Evangelicalism but didn't convert until he was well into his mid-twenties. He was, however, active in politics, becoming a member of Parliament as an independent actor. Other MPs had no love for Wilberforce, as he would frequently flop between supporting individual acts and decisions by both the Tories and the Whigs, which they saw as fence-sitting and a lack of proper commitment. Wilberforce's reasoning had always been to focus on the best decision rather than supporting a particular party's line. The MPs liked him even less when he began to proselytize Evangelical dogma, as religious enthusiasm was extremely frowned upon.

Because of his fresh Evangelical beliefs, as well as a push by some of his compatriots at the time, Wilberforce began to advocate for the abolition of slavery in the British Empire. He would live to learn that the government was going to pass the Bill for the Abolition of Slavery on July 26th, 1833, dying exactly three days later. A mere month after his passing, the House of Lords officially passed the Slavery Abolition Act. Many people in Parliament openly praised Wilberforce for his efforts on this front, and the act had, in effect, been the greatest tribute to his work.

Regarding the East India Company, Wilberforce was an ardent advocate of allowing Evangelical missionaries to proselytize throughout the subcontinent, an action that the Company actively prevented because of the possible rebellions of local Hindu and Muslim subjects. Wilberforce had openly criticized some aspects of Hinduism, such as sati, polygamy, the caste system, and infanticide, but he was also not above criticizing the Company's British officers themselves, pointing to their own hypocrisy and racial prejudices toward the locals.

Statue of William Wilberforce in front of the Wilberforce House on High Street, Hull[xiv]

Keith D at en.wikipedia, CC BY-SA 3.0 <http://creativecommons.org/licenses/by-sa/3.0/>, via Wikimedia Commons

Conclusion

As a political entity, the East India Company had its fair share of ups and downs, of salient, logical moves, and extreme paradoxes. The consequences of its existence can be felt throughout the world, well beyond the isle of Britain and the Indian subcontinent. It was thanks to the actors of the EIC that imperial Britain was to come to the forefront, conquering vast areas of the known world to the point where it was "the empire on which the sun never sets." Most of the atrocities that the Company's directors, writers, secretaries, and governors committed would shed light on the horror that can happen with too much political power, but more importantly, their business dealings would illustrate just how corrupt the powers-that-be were at the time. No individual was fully innocent during the three centuries of the EIC's existence, and each parliamentary action played out like a lackluster farce.

On the Indian side of things, depending on whom you asked, the local princes, rajas, peshwas, ranis, and shahs were either terrible despots with tribal tendencies and brutal customs or innocent victims that fell prey to the white European conquerors. The truth is, of course, far more complex than either of those claims. On the one hand, it's undeniable that the people of India suffered the worst of all throughout the Company's existence. Most of the soldiers that died during the many wars on the subcontinent that were in the Company's service were Indian men. More importantly, the locals would be displaced internally based on the whims of the traders or their local princely allies. Famine and poverty were an everyday occurrence, and though they were technically free to practice their native religions, the people of the subcontinent could have those rights yanked away at any given moment. But the highborn were not treated any better either. Most of them would end up as puppets of the EIC, either through excessive debt or because of an agreement that saw the Company fighting at their side or financing their war endeavors. Entire countries would disappear in a heartbeat due to the Company's ever-increasing military presence.

Looking at the other side, the local rulers were equally capable of heinous acts based purely on interest. It wouldn't be all that rare that a prince would ally himself with the Company in order to crush a neighboring state. While the Company was in its infancy, the local lords would frequently use their positions of power to impose high taxes and appropriate anything they deemed illegal at the time. Even during wartime, different leaders would act in various ways; some would spare their hostages or release them, while others were not beneath killing British women, children, and the elderly. In this respect, the Indian subcontinent was no different than other major regions of conflict throughout history, such as the ancient Middle East or the medieval Balkans.

But despite all of these negative aspects, the East India Company did contribute to the overall world culture in a few positive ways. For instance, there weren't too many enterprises at the time where a commoner could rise to power and become wealthy through free trade. Early signs of entrepreneurship came from the British merchants who risked life and limb to get to a continent they knew next to nothing about. In addition, thanks to some independent actors, the West got a chance to learn about the historical, cultural, and societal backgrounds of the East, and many people became enthusiasts of various Indian and Chinese goods and customs.

Finally, it did give the British one of their favorite pastime traditions—drinking tea in the afternoon.

Two hundred fifty-eight years is a long time for any entity to exist. Whole civilizations have been known to crumble before even a quarter of that time would pass. But for a little over two and a half centuries, India became the training ground for the British Empire, and it all started with a few merchant ships whose crews wanted to trade in the Indian Ocean.

Here are two other books by Captivating History that we think you would find interesting

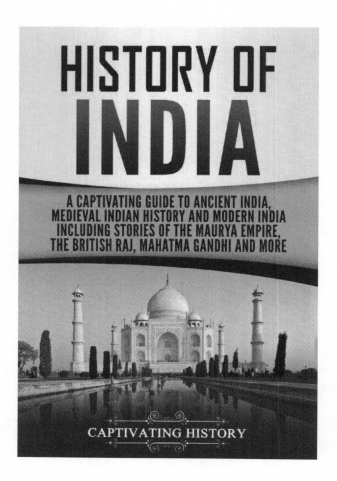

HISTORY OF INDIA

A CAPTIVATING GUIDE TO ANCIENT INDIA, MEDIEVAL INDIAN HISTORY AND MODERN INDIA INCLUDING STORIES OF THE MAURYA EMPIRE, THE BRITISH RAJ, MAHATMA GANDHI AND MORE

CAPTIVATING HISTORY

Bibliography and References

Barrow, I. (2017): *The East India Company 1600-1858: A Short History with Documents*. Indianapolis, IN, USA: Hacket Publishing Company, Inc.

Barbour, R. (2008): The East India Company Journal of Anthony Marlowe, 1607-1608, In *Huntington Library Quarterly* Vol. 71, No. 2, (pp. 255-301). Berkley, CA, USA: University of California Press

Bever Platt, V. (1969): The East India Company and the Madagascar Slave Trade, In *The William and Mary Quarterly, Third Series* Vol. 26, No. 4, (pp. 548-577). Williamsburg, VA, USA: Omohundro Institute of Early American History and Culture

Encyclopedia Britannica (1981), Retrieved on June 18th 2019, from https://www.britannica.com

Finn, M. and Smith, K. (2018): *The East India Company at Home, 1757-1857*. London, UK: UCL Press

Foster, W. (1904): Charles I and the East India Company, In *The English Historical Review* Vol. 19, No. 75, (pp. 456-463). Oxford, UK: Oxford University Press

Harris, A. L. (1964): John Stuart Mill: Servant of the East India Company, In *The Canadian Journal of Economics and Political Science / Revue canadienne d'Economique et de Science politique,* Vol. 30, No. 2, (pp. 185-202). Hoboken, NJ, USA & Vancouver, BC, Canada: Wiley, on behalf of Canadian Economics Association

Hejeebu, S. (2005): Contract Enforcement in the English East India Company, In *The Journal of Economic History* Vol. 65, No. 2, (pp. 89-108). Cambridge, UK & La Crosse, WI, USA: Cambridge University Press, on behalf of the Economic History Association

Johnston, J. M. C. (1903): Coinage of the East India Company, In *The Numismatic Chronicle and Journal of the Numismatic Society, Fourth Series* Vol. 3, (pp. 71-78). London, UK: Royal Numismatic Society

Keay, J. (1991): *The Honourable Company: A History of the English East India Company.* London, UK: HarperCollins Publishers

Marshal, P. J. (1997): Society in India under the East India Company, In *Modern Asian Studies* Vol. 31, No. 1, (pp. 89-108). Cambridge, UK: Cambridge University Press

Matsukata, F. (2016): Contacting Japan: East India Company Letters to the Shogun, In *The Dutch and English East India Companies* (pp. 79-98). Amsterdam, The Netherlands: Amsterdam University Press

Meier Schleisinger, A. (1917): The Uprising against the East India Company, In *Political Science Quarterly* Vol. 32, No. 1, (pp. 60-79). New York City, NY, USA: Academy of Political Science

Phillips, C. H. (1940): The Secret Committee of the East India Company, In *Bulletin of the School of Oriental Studies University of London* Vol. 10, No. 2, (pp. 299-315). Cambridge, UK: Cambridge University Press

Wikipedia (January 15, 2001), Retrieved on June 18th 2019, from https://www.wikipedia.org/

Notes on Images

[i] Original image uploaded by Yaddah on 4 June 2006. Retrieved from https://commons.wikimedia.org/ on November 2019 under the following license: *Public Domain*. This item is in the public domain, and can be used, copied, and modified without any restrictions.

[ii] Original image uploaded by Luis wiki on 12 March 2011. Retrieved from https://commons.wikimedia.org/ on November 2019 under the following license: Creative Commons Attribution-ShareAlike 2.5 Generic. This license lets others remix, tweak, and build upon your work even for commercial reasons, as long as they credit you and license their new creations under the identical terms.

[iii] Original image uploaded by Prioryman on 30 January 2015. Retrieved from https://commons.wikimedia.org/ on November 2019 under the following license: Creative Commons Attribution-ShareAlike 4.0 International. This license lets others remix, tweak, and build upon your work even for commercial reasons, as long as they credit you and license their new creations under the identical terms.

[iv] Original image uploaded by William Maury Morris II on 16 September 2016. Retrieved from https://commons.wikimedia.org/ on November 2019 under the following license: *Public Domain*. This item is in the public domain, and can be used, copied, and modified.

[v] Original image uploaded by Taterian on 23 October 2017. Retrieved from https://commons.wikimedia.org/ on November 2019 under the following license: *Public Domain*. This item is in the public domain, and can be used, copied, and modified.

[vi] Original image uploaded by Sridhar1000 on 17 March 2012. Retrieved from https://commons.wikimedia.org/ on November 2019 under the following license: *Public Domain*. This item is in the public domain, and can be used, copied, and modified.

[vii] Original image uploaded by Godot13 on 13 February 2015. Retrieved from https://commons.wikimedia.org/ on November 2019 under the following license: *Public Domain*. This item is in the public domain, and can be used, copied, and modified.

[viii] Original image uploaded by Santosh.mbahrm on 26 September 2015. Retrieved from https://commons.wikimedia.org/ on November 2019 under the following license: Creative Commons Attribution-ShareAlike 3.0 Unported. This license lets

others remix, tweak, and build upon your work even for commercial reasons, as long as they credit you and license their new creations under the identical terms.

[ix] Original image uploaded by Pratishkhedekar on 2 January 2019. Retrieved from https://commons.wikimedia.org/ on November 2019 under the following license: *Public Domain*. This item is in the public domain, and can be used, copied, and modified.

[x] Original image uploaded by Themadchopper on 9 October 2017. Retrieved from https://commons.wikimedia.org/ on November 2019 under the following license: *Public Domain*. This item is in the public domain, and can be used, copied, and modified.

[xi] Original image uploaded by Sridhar1000 on 5 April 2012. Retrieved from https://commons.wikimedia.org/ on November 2019 under the following license: *Public Domain*. This item is in the public domain, and can be used, copied, and modified.

[xii] Original image uploaded by Ficusindica on 13 January 2012. Retrieved from https://commons.wikimedia.org/ on November 2019 under the following license: *Public Domain*. This item is in the public domain, and can be used, copied, and modified.

[xiii] Original image uploaded by Gonzaga 28-08 on 2 October 2014. Retrieved from https://commons.wikimedia.org/ on November 2019 under the following license: *Public Domain*. This item is in the public domain, and can be used, copied, and modified.

[xiv] Original image uploaded by WonRyong on 14 June 2008. Retrieved from https://commons.wikimedia.org/ on November 2019 under the following license: Creative Commons Attribution-ShareAlike 3.0 Unported. This license lets others remix, tweak, and build upon your work even for commercial reasons, as long as they credit you and license their new creations under the identical terms.

Made in the USA
Middletown, DE
17 February 2023

25121534R00047